I0151699

Fruit of the Spirit;
Words of Wisdom

By: Bernice Anita Quinn-Williams

I would like to thank God for the blessing and gift to write. I would like to dedicate this book to my sons Zachariah and Joshua with all of my love forever and always.

Table of Contents

Title	Page
Set Up, Set Out, Let God Have Full Control	1
Wilderness	3
Devotion	4
Heaven	5
The Meaning of the Gospel	6
Directions	7
Living for Christ	8
Gracious	9
Faithful	10
Tithes	11
Heart of Love	12
Worthy	13
Praise Him	14
Fear	15
God	16
Hold to the Word	17
Consult God	18
God Looks At Your Heart	19
Grow	20
Open The Door	21
Honor Your Word	22
Jesus Is Lord	23
Pure Light	24
Use Your Heart	25
Fortress	26
Communion	27
Purified	28
Peace of God	29

Righteous Judge   30
Plan for Life   31
Divine Health   32
Receive   33
Beside the Lord   34
Son   35
Give
Gift
Plea   36
Unity
Encounter Your Victory   37
Winning Attitude   38
Loving the Lord   39
Opening his Arms   40
Miracle for You   41
Inseparable   42
Blessing   43
Increase   44
Word   45
Praise   46
Dance
Free   47
Trial
Church   48
Grace
Mercy
Count Your Victory   49
Heart   50
Tear
Love on Jesus   51
Promise Land   52
Hammer Nails   53

Justified   54
Conqueror   55
Born of God   56
Door To Prosperity   57
Peace   58
Glory
Hearing the Voice   59
Holy   60
Intercession   61
Yield Ability to God   62
Be a Blessing   63
Strong Tower   64
Fullness of God   65
My Harvest   66
Goodness of God   67
Testimony   68
Obedience   69
Know God's Word   70
Love   71
Empower   72
Authority   73
Committed   74
Hope   75
Strength
Rain   76
Portion   77
Eternal Life   78
Shield of Faith   79
Relationship   80
Labor   81
Freedom
Mount Up   82

Service   83
Ministry   84
Feet on Fire   85
Lead You to Success   86
Petitions   87
Fear the Lord   88
Harvest with a Seed   89
My Seed Meets My Needs   90

Set Up, Set Out, Let God Have Full Control

Speaking

Every

Time

Upward to Jesus Christ

Pleasing God

Sacrifice

Everything

Together

Of

Understanding

The Word

Leading

Eternal life of

Thanksgiving

Giving

Offerings of

Dedication

Helping

All of

Victory

Every time

Fullness

Uttering

Lovely

Lips of Praises

Continue

Of

New

Testimony

Releasing

Only Love for God

<u>Wilderness</u>

Walking into

Loyal

Devotion for

Everlasting

Reassurance

Never

Empty of

Sacrifices from our

Savior

<u>Devotion</u>

Dedicated

Each

Victory

Offering

Thanksgiving

Into

Our

New Praise

<u>Heaven</u>

Higher for

Eternal life

Always receiving

Victory

Every time to make

New songs to praise him!

The Meaning of the Gospel

Praying for each other

Reaching for guidance

Everlasting touch of his hand

Accepting you as you are

Coaching you all the way through

Helping in all you do

Thanksgiving of his blessings

Healing of your body

Eternal life

Giving of himself

Opening his arms

Sacrificed his son

Pleasing all of the time

Every time you call on him, he's there

Living forever in his love

<u>Directions</u>

Dedication

Involving

Reaping

Each

Connection

Toward

Intercession

Obedience

Needing our

Savior

Living for Christ

Loving you

Intercessory prayer

Victory in blessings

In all you do

Needing him at all times

Giving of himself

Forgiving

Others for the

Repentance of their sins

Carriers all of your burdens

Helping hand

Risen Savior

Involvement of your life

Saving souls

Touching others while living for Christ!

<u>Gracious</u>

Grace

Reaching

Avenues of help

Crying before our Father of having

Intercessory prayers to

Overcome which

Uphold

Sacrifices

<u>Faithful</u>

Fruit of

Anointed words

Including

Truth

Healing by the

Father of his

Undying

Love

<u>Tithes</u>

Testimony

Intercession

Together

Healing

Each

Soul

Heart of Love

Helping

Each other

Achieve to

Reach

The Lord

Offering our

Father

Lips

Of abundant praises of

Victory

Every day

<u>Worthy</u>

Word

Of

Receiving

Truth

Helping

You daily

Praise Him

Pleasing

Releasing

All

Increasing

Songs of praise

Every day

Holy

Involving harmony words

Making praises to the Lord

<u>Fear</u>

Face

Every day of

Aspects

Reaching to higher calling

<u>God</u>

Giving

Obedience on a

Daily basis to his word

Hold to the Word

Helping

Offering

Leading

Deliverance

Toward

Others

Through

Hearing

Each

Word

On each

Renewing

Day

Consult God

Carrying

Our

Needs

Seeking our Father

Using our

Light

Talking to

God by

Obedience of

Deliverance

God Looks At Your Heart

Greatness of

Obedience of

Dedication

Loving

Our Father

Of

Knowing the

Son

Awesome

Thoughts

Yielding

Of

Ushering

Respect

Hearing

Each Aspect Releasing

Thanksgiving of Praise!

<u>Grow</u>

Gather

Reap of

Owning the

Word of your instructions to life

Open The Door

Offering

Patience

Every day

Needing

The Lord to

Help

Each Soul on a

Daily basis to

Open windows

Of

Rescuing you from harm

Honor Your Word

Helping

Of

Needing

Our

Respect of hearing

You're Voice

Of

Using the

Receiving instructions

Willing to
Observe

Repentance for

Deliverance

Jesus Is Lord

Justify

Everything

Saving

Us from our

Sins

Inward

Sacrifice

Living through

Obstacles

Receiving

Daily blessings

Pure Light

Precious

Unity

Reassurance in

Every word

Living

In

Greatness

Highly

Thanks for his pure light

Use Your Heart

Understand the

Sacrifice for

Everything

You accomplish

Open

Up to

Receive

Hands of blessings

Each day

Aiming to

Reach

The LORD!

Fortress

Falling

On our knees to

Repent of our sins

Telling of

Receiving

Each blessing by the

Sacrifice for the

Son, JESUS CHRIST!

Communion

Calling

On

Making

Ministry of

Unity by

Needing

Intercession

On each

New day

<u>Purified</u>

Praise

Unity

Releasing

Intercession through

Faith

Inward

Every

Day

Peace of God

Precious of

Each

Awesome

Calling of

Every word

Of

Following

Greatness

Of our

Deliverer

Righteous Judge

Reach

Inward of

Gathering and

Having

Thanks

Every day by

Order

Unto the

Savior when he

Justifies you, through and

Under the

Deliverance of

Getting

Eternal Life!

Plan for Life

Pray

Leaning

At all times

Needing our

Father

Obeying

Receiving

Love

Inward

Living for

Eternal Life

Divine Health

Deliverance

Inward

Victory of

Intercessory words

Needing him

Each day

Helping

Each other

Allowing the

Lord to

Touch our souls for our

Health to be divine

<u>Receive</u>

Rescue

Each

Child

Every moment

In

Various times

Every day

Beside the Lord

Believing in

Everlasting love

Soul satisfied because of

Intercessory prayer for

Deliverance of our sins for

Eternal life

Taking his word of

Helping others

Every day

Living

Out the

Repentance to be a true

Devotion

Son

Soul

Of

Needs, which our Savior fulfills

Give

Greatness

Importance

Victory

Every time

Gift

Gracious

In our

Father for

Thanksgiving

Plea

Pardon

Living

Each day

A new life

Unity

Unto

Never leaving you

Into our

Testimonies

Yielding to him daily

Encounter Your Victory

Each Need to Carry by

Our Father, through

Understanding the

New blessings

Together of

Every word by the

Repentance of

Your sins

Offering words of

Utterance of praise

Receiving eternal life

Various

Inward

Commitments of

Thoughts of

Obedience

Releasing words

Yielding to our FATHER!

Winning Attitude

Words

In

New sayings

Never the same

Involving and

Needing to pray

Going before the Lord

Allowing

Trials and

Tribulations through

Intercession

Talking to Jesus Christ

Using praises of

Dedication to have

Eternal life

Loving the Lord

Living for him

Obeying his word

Victory in praise

Involved in your daily life

Never leaving you

Giving of himself

Touching your life

Helping you through for

Eternal Life

Loving you at all times

Obedience in what you say

Receiving your blessings

Dedicated by loving the LORD!

Opening his Arms

Offering his love

Pleasing in his touch

Everlasting memories

Never leaving you

Involved in your daily walk

Need to accept his love

Giving all of the time

Helping you through

Intercessory prayer

Saving your soul

Accepting you as you are

Rescuing you from harm

Making time for you

Securing you by opening his arms

Miracle for You

Marvelous words

Intercessory Prayers

Reassurance by praising him

Always by your side

Count your blessings

Love you forever

Everlasting love

Faith in God

Obey his voice

Rescuing you from trials and tribulations

Yielding to our father

Our souls being saved

Unity as one

Inseparable

Inspiring Father

Needing to be on our knees before him

Sacrificed his son for

Eternal life

Partaker of his word

Always by your side

Revealing through the Holy Spirit

Awesome in his touch

Believer forever

Loving Savior of giving

Everlasting love

Blessing

Beloved Father

Leaning on his word

Eternal life for the

Sacrifice of his

Son, which he gave

Inward of the heart brings

Notions, which flow

Given, known as a blessing

Increase

Intercession prayer

Needing him to

Carry and

Rescue you by

Each plea

At all times

Seeking

Each soul

<u>Word</u>

Wisdom

Of

Receiving

Directions

<u>Praise</u>

Prayer of

Returning

Acts

In

Sacrifices of

Everyone praises

<u>Dance</u>

Dedicated

Awesome

Needing him

Committed to

Each soul

Free

Freedom

Receiving

Eternal life

Every day

Trial

Times of

Repenting

In

Areas of your

Life daily

Church

Calling

Helping

Usher

Respect to

Chosen souls everyday

Helping them to be saved

Grace

God shows us

Remembering all of his

Awesome obedient

Children with his

Everlasting love, which is grace!

Mercy

Memories of calling

Every time I need to

Receive some type of

Courage from God

Yielding to him

Count Your Victory

Call

On the Lord

Understanding

New

Times

Yielding up to

Our Savior by

Upholding

Reverence through

Various

Intercession

Carrying our

Trials and Tribulations

Offering and Giving

Respect by praising

Your Father, to Count Your Victory!

<u>Heart</u>

Hearing

Each

Ache

Reaping

Through praises to our Father

<u>Tear</u>

Together

Each

Avenue of

Returning back to him!

<u>Love on Jesus</u>

Living

Only for

Victory to have

Everything

Of

Never leaving you

Justify

Each

Soul of

Understanding our

Savior!

Promise Land

Praise

Receiving

Obedience

Making

Inward of

Saving

Each soul

Loving

Always

Needing our

Devoted Father!

Hammer Nails

Helping

As our

Master

Maker gave

Everlasting

Repentance for our sins

Needing and

Asking to have

Intercession for

Love to feed our

Souls

Justified

Joy

Understanding the

Sacrifice

Telling

Involving

Faithful praises

In

Everything for my

Destiny

<u>Conqueror</u>

Calling

On the

Need of

Quick

Understanding of

Each

Release

Of

Rewards

Born of God

Believe

Only

Receiving the Redemption

Needing

Our

Father

Gathering and Giving

Our

Devotions, a daily promise

Door to Prosperity

Doing his will

Opening the door

Of

Receiving blessings

Toward

Others

Praising and

Releasing rewards

Of

Souls

Pleasing to have

Eternal life

Reaching through

Intercessory

Together

Yielding to Our Lord

Peace

Preach

Every time

Awesome

Commitment of words

Exalt his holy name

Glory

Giving

Love

Offering and

Receiving grace through

You, the FATHER!

Hearing the Voice

Help

Every

Act

Repenting

In

Needing

God

Thanking Jesus for

Helping

Each of us in our

Victory

Of

Intercession

Choosing

Eternal life

<u>Holy</u>

Higher calling through

Obedience in

Love

Yielding to his instructions

Intercession

In life

Never leaving us

Talking

Every day

Receiving

Choices for

Each

Spoken words

Saving lives

Involving

One saying

Needing him, while we pray=INTERCESSION

<u>Yield Ability to God</u>

Yes

In

Each

Living

Day

Always
Blessing

Inward

Letting

Intercession make

Testimony

Yielding

To

Our

God, the Father

Of

Delivering a message

Be a Blessing

Believing

Each day

Awesome of

Building

Love just to have

Eternal life by God

Sacrificing his

Son

In all of our lives

Never

Giving up the fight

Strong Tower

Study

The

Reading

Of

Needing the

Gift of Instructions

Telling

Our

Words

Each day

Receiving blessings

Fullness of God

Following and

Understand the

Love of the

Lord

Never out of nothing

Everything

Saving

Souls

Of our

Faith by

God

Offering

Deliverance

My Harvest

Marvelous

Yielding to his voice

Hearing from

Above

Receiving

Visions

Every times our

Savior

Touches, your soul

Goodness of God

Greatness

Of

Offering up

Dedications being

New

Every day to

Sacrifice our

Soul to have

Obedience of

Faith

Greatly for

Our life to give

Daily devotions

<u>Testimony</u>

Touching

Each

Soul

Telling

Interesting blessings which

Make

Obedience that we

Need from our Father

Yearning, for his LOVE!

Obedience

Owning

Believing of receiving

Eternal life because

Dedication to Christ

Intercession

Every day

Needing

Chances to stay right

Each moment we live

Know God's Word

Keeping

Now to

Open the

Word for

Glory

Of
Devine

Strength

Which

Offer

Reassuring

Deliverance

<u>Love</u>

Living

Our

Victory

Every day

Empower

Everlasting

Memories

Pleasing

Our Father

With

Eternal life

Resting in HEAVEN!!!

<u>Authority</u>

All

Understand

Through

His

Overwhelming

Repentance

In

Thoughts of

Yielding to him

<u>Committed</u>

Counting and

Offering

Marvelous

Moments

Involving

Trials and

Tribulations giving

Every blessing a

Devotion of praise

<u>Hope</u>

Hearing

Our

Purpose for

Eternal Life

<u>Strength</u>

Savior

Touching

Releasing

Enough to our

Needs of

Gathering

To

Heal lost souls

<u>Rain</u>

Reaching

Always

Interceding

Needing Christ!

Portion

Prayer

Of

Releasing

Thoughts

In and

Of the

Name, JESUS CHRUST!

Eternal Life

Everlasting love

Together forever

Every day with you

Reassurance in his word

Never giving up

Accepting you as you are

Loving you, with open arms

Living victory

In harmony at all times

Forever knowing you have

Eternal life!

Shield of Faith

Salvation

Healing

Involvement

Everlasting

Life

Dedicated to God

Offering his love

For us

Faith in our Lord

Awesome in his word

Intercessory prayer

Truthful MASTER!

Having him in your life forever

Relationship

Release

Each

Letter

At all

Times

In

Our

Needed

Souls for

Help through

Intercessory

Prayer

Labor

Love

At

Birth

Of

Receiving your gift, your child!

Freedom

Faith being

Released

Each and

Every

Day, from

Our

MASTER!

Mount Up

Marvelous

Obedience

Understand his word

Never let go

Together with my FATHER!

Upward speaking

Petitions before him to mount up

<u>Service</u>

Serving

Every time

Releasing

Victorious of

Intercession

Choosing

Eternal life

Ministry

Message

In

Needing every word

Involving

Scriptures

Trusting and

Rescuing

You with his blessings

Feet on Fire

Faith of having

Eternal life going through

Enough

Trials and Tribulations

Offering up praises

Needing him to bless

Facing him through

Intercessory prayer

Rescuing you with his instructions

Every day

<u>Lead You to Success</u>

Leading

Excitement

At

Devotions

You

Offer

Unto

Toward

Our

Savior

Uttering

Commitment

Carrying

Every

Saying for your

Success

<u>Petitions</u>

Prepare

Every

Thought for

Intercessory prayer

Talking about the

Instructions

On our behalf

Needing our Savior, for our

Souls to be feed

Fear the Lord

Faith in God

Everything you go through

Awesome in his touch

Rescue you from harm

Thanksgiving in praising

Him

Every day by

Loving through

Obedience

Receiving

Daily blessings!

Harvest with a Seed

Heart

Always

Receiving

Victory

Each

Sacrifice

Toward our Father

Worship

In the

Truth

Having the understanding

Aiming to

Seek the word

Each and

Every

Day

My Seed Meets My Needs

Magnify

Yearning for our

Savior

Every moment of

Each

Day

Making choices for

Each of us to have

Eternal life

Touching our

Souls

Marvelous harvest

Yielding to our Father

Needing him in

Everything I do

Every day

Dedicated to the

Son, who saved our souls!

www.ingramcontent.com/pod-product-compliance
Lightning Source LLC
LaVergne TN
LVHW021613080426
835510LV00019B/2549